Trapped!

by Griselda Gifford
Illustrated by Beryl Sanders

CONTENTS

STECK-VAUGHN
C O M P A N Y

Chapter 1: Nowhere to Play

It was a wet day. Ben and his friend Max were playing in the living room. There were cars all over the floor. Ben's train set was laid out. The lines went under the chairs and a pile of books made a tunnel. Comics were mixed up with blocks. The boys had built a camp out of a chair, a table and a blanket. They sat inside eating crackers.

Ben saw Mom's feet as she came into the room. Now there would be trouble!

"What a mess!" she said. "You must clean it up at once! Why don't you play in your bedroom, Ben?"

"It's too small to lay out the train set," said Ben. "And it's too wet to go out. We must have somewhere to play."

"Sorry, but you will have to clean it up all the same," Mom said.

Mom went back to work in the card shop
she ran with Ben's father. They sold
newspapers, cards, and stationery.
They lived in an apartment above the shop.
   Max lived in the house next door.
His parents had a grocery store.
They lived in the rooms above the store.
Max also had very little room for playing.
His mother always made him put his toys away.

The boys took down the camp and
put away the train set. They knocked down
the garages and the tunnel they had built.

"Where can we play?" asked Max.

Ben brushed the cracker crumbs under the sofa.

"I know!" he said. "Let's go up to the roof!"
Ben always had the ideas.

Chapter 2: The Secret Camp

"We can't climb on the roof," Max said.

"No! We will go up into the attic," Ben said. "There is a ladder. Come on!"

Ben ran into the hall. The ladder to the attic was hooked up to the ceiling of the hall. Ben stood on a chair and unhooked it. He pulled the ladder down.

"What about your Mom and Dad?" asked Max. "Do they let you go up to the attic?"

"They will be busy until the shop closes," said Ben. "They won't know. It will be our secret place."

"Our attic is full of junk," said Max. "Nobody goes up there."

Ben went up the ladder first. The trap door was heavy to push up. At last it opened and fell back.

Ben climbed into the attic. Max followed him. They looked around. The attic had one small window. There were a lot of cobwebs. The heater rumbled on one side. Boxes were stacked against the wall between the two houses. The light was dim. It was a good place for a secret camp.

Ben had once been to the attic with his dad.
His dad had said he was not to go there alone.
Well, he wasn't alone with Max, was he?

   Parts of the floor were boarded over.
The rest was just wooden beams with
plaster underneath. Dad had said it was easy
to make a hole in the plaster.

"We can make a camp on the boarded part,"
Ben said. "I will get my cars. There isn't very much room,
but we can leave the toys up here."

They got the cars, the blocks, and the comics.

"I know," said Ben. "I will write a note saying
I am playing with you at your house, Max.
Then if they come upstairs they won't know
I am in the attic."

"Good idea," said Max.

Ben wrote the note and left it on the hall table.

Chapter 3: Waiting for Max

"We need food," said Max. "I'll go and get some crackers, drinks, nuts, and fruit from my house."

"Then we can stay in the attic for a long time," said Ben, who was always hungry. "Before you go, I will take the toys up into the attic," he said. "Then you bolt the trap door and hook the ladder up. Our place will be secret then."

Max bolted the trap door and went to his house. "I won't be long," he called out.

Ben put the cars on the attic floor. He built
a garage with the blocks.

Max was gone a long time. Ben felt hungry.
He looked out of the small window. It was dirty
and covered with cobwebs. It was raining
outside in the street.

Ben thought he saw Max's dad's van
going down the street. It turned the corner
and was gone. He sighed. Where was Max?
It was boring here on his own.
He tried to read a comic book by the window.
Surely Max would come soon? He listened
for footsteps. Nothing happened.

Ben wondered if Max had forgotten all about him.
Perhaps his mother would not let him come back.
Ben's parents would not know where he was.
They would think he was with Max.

Ben was very hungry now. He might starve
up here before they heard him call out.
He couldn't unbolt the trap door from inside.

Chapter 4: Trapped!

Even if the trap door was open, he would have to jump a long way down. Ben told himself he was too old to cry. After all, his parents must come upstairs when the shop was closed. Perhaps if he knocked loudly someone might hear.

He banged on the trap door. "Help!" he called. "I'm stuck up here! Mom! Dad!"

Nobody came. It was just after lunch. It would be hours until the shop closed.

Why didn't Max come back? Ben went to
the little window. Perhaps if he waved and
called someone might see him. He waved but
nobody looked up. How foolish he had been!
It was silly letting himself be shut in.

Suppose there was a fire? Nobody would know
he was there.

Perhaps he could find another way out.
Ben walked around the attic. When he came to
the end of the boarded part, he was careful
only to step on the wooden beams. He did not want
to fall through.

Just to keep himself from crying, he moved some
of the boxes. They were filled with old clothes,
saucepans, and baby toys. Here was his old bed,
behind the boxes. Here was his baby bathtub.
He could not believe he had ever been
small enough to lie in the bed or the tub.

He wondered if he should move all the boxes
to find another way out of the attic.
Then he saw some different colored paint.
He moved another box.

There was a square of dirty paint covered
in cobwebs. He looked closer. It was a door!
Nobody had opened it for a long time.

The door had a rusty bolt. It must lead to
Max's attic. Ben tried to move the bolt, but
it was stuck.

Chapter 5: Escape

    Ben was so disappointed that he did cry, just a little.
Mom always said: "If at first you don't succeed,
try, try again." Well, he would try again.

    He wriggled and pushed at the bolt. At last
he felt it move, just a little. If only he had some oil.

    He gave a big tug. The bolt shot back.
He went through the little door into the next attic.

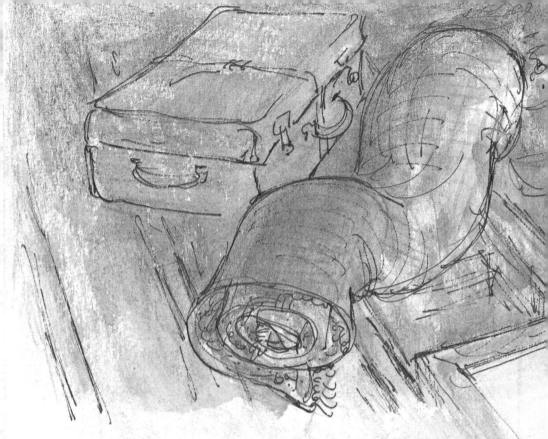

Max's attic was full of junk, just as Max had said.
Ben saw boxes and cases and rolls of old carpet.
The only light came through a little piece of glass
in the roof. Nobody had put boards on this floor.
It was all beams. He walked along them carefully until
he came to a trap door like the one in his attic.

Perhaps nobody would hear him. Perhaps
Max's parents had closed the store and
they had all gone out.

"Help!" he called. "Max, where are you?
It's your fault I'm shut in!"

Nobody came.

He took off his shoe and banged on the trap door.
He banged and banged until his arm ached.
Again he nearly cried. Then suddenly he heard a voice.

"Who's that?" called Max's dad.

"It's me! It's Ben!" Ben called.

He heard a clattering. Then the bolt was opened.

The trap door was flung back. It knocked him
off the beams. One of his feet went through the plaster.

"Oh!" cried Ben. He could not move!
One leg had disappeared up to his knee!

"My ceiling!" said Max's dad. He came up
into the attic. He pulled Ben free and
helped him down the ladder.

"Look what happened," he said.

Ben saw the hole in the bathroom ceiling.
Pieces of plaster lay on the floor.

"I'm sorry," Ben said. "But I was shut in our attic.
I found a door to yours. Where's Max?"

"His Gran was taken to the hospital," said Max's father.
"Max went with his mom to see her.
What were you doing in the attic?"

"Well, we had nowhere to play," Ben said.
"That's why we went to our attic."

"I think you had better run home quickly,"
said Max's father. "Your mother
has been here to look for you. I said
you had not been in the house."

Ben was worried. She might have called the police.

Chapter 6: A Great Idea!

Ben met his mother on their doorstep.
She was wearing a raincoat.

"I have been to the park to look for you," she said.
They went through the shop.

"I'm sorry," Ben said. He told her what
had happened.

"You told a lie in your note," Mom said.
"It would have served you right if you had
stayed up in the attic until dinner."

Ben's father was angry when he heard that
Ben had put his foot through the ceiling next door.

"I will go and see Max's father when my shop
has closed," he said. "And you can come with me."

He gave Ben jobs to do in the shop until it closed
instead of watching TV.

"That's your punishment!" he said.

Later they went to Max's house. Max and his mother
were just getting out of the van. Max stood still.
His mouth opened.

"Oh Ben!" he said. "I was so worried about my Gran.
I forgot about you!"

"I found a door from your attic to mine," Ben said.

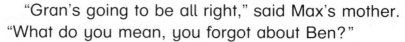

"Gran's going to be all right," said Max's mother. "What do you mean, you forgot about Ben?"

They went inside and everyone explained all over again. Ben's father looked at the hole in the bathroom ceiling.

"It's a good thing you have a small foot," Dad said. "I shall come and put more plaster on the ceiling and then paint it," he said to Max's father.

"It was silly to go up into the attic," Mom said.

"There is no room in our house to play," Ben said. "And you don't like me to leave my train set out."

"There's no room in our house, either," said Max.

"Both attics would be great playrooms," said Ben.

"Perhaps they do need more space to play," said Ben's father.

"Yes," agreed Max's parents.

"We are all so busy with our shops," said Ben's mother. "There's no time to pick up toys all day."

"It would mean clearing out all those boxes," said Max's mother.

"We could board over the floor in both attics," said Ben's father.

"Then nobody could fall through!" Max's mother laughed. Ben thought it was kind of her when she had a hole in her bathroom ceiling.

"And they will need electricity," said Max's father.

"We can help," Ben said.

"Yes, of course we can," said Max.

"It's a great idea!" said Ben.

The boys helped all they could.
They brushed away the cobwebs and the dirt.
They helped put the boards on the floors
over the beams. They helped take down
the old boxes and sort out the junk.
Ben's father made the little window open.
   "It will be hot up here in the summer," he said.
   The fathers wired the attic for electricity.
It took some time because they still had to
work in their shops.

At last it was done. Ben's mom made a cake. Max brought crackers and fruit from the store. Ben brought up comics from his parents' shop.

They took up the blocks, the toy cars, and Max's model airplanes. They went up the ladder with puzzles. Now they did not have to be put away when they were finished. They took up their water pistols. Now nobody would mind about the splashes!

   Last of all, they arranged the two electric
train sets on the floor. They could hook up
the lines now. Ben's joined Max's through
the open door between the attics.
   "We can send messages by train to each other,"
said Ben.
   "No more mess!" said their mothers.
   "I can play my music loudly up here,"
said Max. "It's great!"
   "It will be really private," said Ben.
He fixed a sign to both ladders:

PRIVATE PROPERTY.
PLEASE KEEP OUT!

When I'm Grown Up

I wonder what I would like to be.
A soldier, perhaps, in the queen's army.

I might be a nurse in an apron white,
To help heal the sick by day and night.

It might be fun to fly a plane,
To swoop to the sky and down again.

Maybe I'll swing on a high trapeze,
Flying above your heads with ease.

Perhaps I'll be a policeman tall,
I'll come and help whenever you call.

Perhaps I'll be a circus clown
Making you laugh when you're feeling down.

Sailors I know go off to sea,
Perhaps a sailor is what I'll be.

A fireman's job is a dangerous one,
For putting out fires is never fun.

There are so many things that I might be,
I'll wait a few years and then I'll see.

Peggy Clulow